WHY GROW OLD?

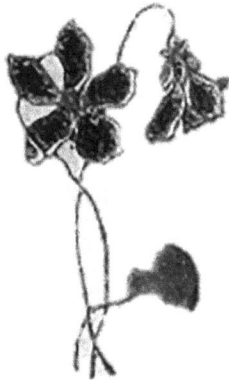

WHY GROW OLD?

Why Grow Old?

By
Orison Swett Marden
Author of "Every Man a King,"
"Peace Power, and Plenty,"
etc.

New York
Thomas Y. Crowell & Co.
Publishers

ISBN: 978-1-6673-0521-9 paperback
ISBN: 978-1-6673-0522-6 hardcover

WHY GROW OLD?

*"The face cannot betray the years until
the mind has given its consent.
The mind is the sculptor,"*

*"We renew our bodies by renewing
our thoughts; change our bodies,
our habits, by changing our thoughts."*

NOT long ago the former secretary to a justice of the New York Supreme Court committed suicide on his seventieth birthday.

"The Statute of Limitations; a Brief Essay on the Osier Theory of Life," was found beside the dead body. It read in part:

"Threescore and ten – this is the scriptural statute of limitations. After that, active work for man ceases, his time on earth has expired. . . .

"I am seventy – threescore and ten – and I am fit only for the chimney-corner. . . ."

This man had dwelt so long on the so-called Osler theory – that a man is practically useless and only a burden to himself and the world after sixty – and the biblical limitation of life to threescore years and ten, that he made up his mind he would end it all on his seventieth birthday.

Leaving aside Dr. Osler's theory, there is no doubt that the acceptance in a strictly literal sense of the biblical life limit has proved a decided injury to the race. We are powerfully influenced by our self-imposed limitations and convictions, and it is well known that many people die very near the limit they set for themselves, even though they are in good health when this conviction settles upon them. Yet there is no probability that the Psalmist had any idea of setting any limit to the life period, or that he had any authority whatever for so doing. Many of the sayings in the Bible which people take so literally and accept blindly as standards of living are merely figures of speech used to illustrate an idea. So far as the Bible is concerned, there is just as much reason for setting the life limit at one hundred and twenty or even at Methuselah's age (nine hundred and sixty-nine) as at seventy or eighty. There is no evidence in the Scriptures that even suggests the existence of an age limit beyond which man was not supposed or allowed to pass.

In fact the whole spirit of the Bible is to encourage long life through sane and healthful living. It points to the duty of living a useful and noble life, of making as much of ourselves as possible, all of which tends to prolong our years on earth.

It would be a reflection upon the Creator to suggest that He would limit human life to less than three times the age at which it reaches maturity (about thirty) when all the analogy of nature, especially in the animal kingdom, points to at least five times the length of the maturing period. Should not the highest manifestation of God's creation have a length of life at least equal to that of the animal? Infinite wisdom does not shake the fruit off the tree before it is ripe.

We do not half realize what slaves we are to our mental attitudes, what power our convictions have to influence our lives. Multitudes of people undoubtedly shorten their lives by many years because of their deep-seated convictions that they will not live beyond a certain age – the age, perhaps, at which their parents died. How often we hear this said: "I do not expect to live to be very old; my father and mother died young."

Not long ago a New York man, in perfect health, told his family that he was certain he should die on his next birthday. On the morning of his birthday his family, alarmed because he refused to go to work, saying that he should certainly die before midnight, insisted upon calling in the family physician, who examined him and said there was nothing the matter with him. But the man refused to eat, grew weaker and weaker during the day, and actually died before midnight. The conviction that he was going to die had become so intrenched in his mind that the whole force of his mentality acted to cut off the life force, and finally to strangle completely the life processes.

Now, if this man's conviction could have been changed by some one who had sufficient power over him, or if the mental suggestion that he was going to live to a good old age had been implanted in his mind in place of the death idea, he would probably have lived many years longer.

If you have convinced yourself, or if the idea has been ingrained into the very structure of your being by your training or the multitudes of examples about you, that you will begin to show the marks of age at about fifty, that at sixty you will lose the power of your faculties, your interest in life; that you will become practically useless and have to retire from your business, and that thereafter you will continue to decline until you are cut off entirely, there is no power in the world that can keep the old-age processes and signs from developing in you.

Thought leads. If it is an old-age thought, old age must follow. If it is a youthful thought, a perennial young-life thought, a thought of usefulness and helpfulness, the body must correspond. Old age begins in the mind. The expression of age in the body is the harvest of old-age ideas which have been planted in the mind. We see others about our age beginning to decline and show marks of decrepitude, and we imagine it is about time for us to show the same signs. Ultimately we do show them, because we think they are inevitable. But they are only inevitable because of our old-age mental attitude and race habit beliefs.

If we actually refuse to grow old; if we insist on holding the youthful ideal and the young, hopeful, buoyant thought, the old-age ear-marks will not show themselves.

The elixir of youth lies in the mind or nowhere.

You cannot be young by trying to appear so, by dressing youthfully. You must first get rid of the last vestige of thought that you are aging. As long as that is in the mind, cosmetics and youthful dress will amount to very little in changing your appearance. The conviction must first be changed; the thought which has produced the aging condition must be reversed.

If we can only establish the perpetual-youth mental attitude, so that we feel young, we have won half the battle against old age. Be sure of this, that whatever you feel regarding your age will be expressed in your body.

It is a great aid to the perpetuation of youth to learn to feel young, however long we may have lived, because the body expresses the habitual feeling, habitual thought. Nothing in the world will make us look young as long as we are convinced that we are aging.

Nothing else more effectually retards age than the keeping in mind the bright, cheerful, optimistic, hopeful, buoyant picture of youth, in all its splendor, magnificence; the picture of the glories which belong to youth – youthful dreams, ideals, hopes, and all the qualities which belong to young life.

One great trouble with us is that our imaginations age prematurely. The hard, exacting conditions of our modern, strenuous life tend to harden and dry up the brain and nerve cells, and thus seriously injure the power of the imagination, which should be kept fresh, bouyant, elastic. The average routine habit of modern business life tends to destroy the flexibility, the delicacy, the sensitiveness, the exquisite fineness of the perceptive faculties.

People who take life too seriously, who seem to think everything depends upon their own individual efforts, whose lives are one continuous grind in living-getting, have a hard expression, their thought outpictures itself in their faces. These people dry up early in life, become wrinkled; their tissues become as hard as their thought.

The arbitrary, domineering, overbearing mind also tends to age the body prematurely, because the thinking is hard, strained, abnormal.

People who live on the sunny and beautiful side of life, who cultivate serenity, do not age nearly so rapidly as do those who live on the shady, the dark side.

Another reason why so many people age prematurely is because they cease to grow. It is a lamentable fact that multitudes of men seem incapable of receiving or accepting new ideas after they have reached middle age. Many of them, after they have reached the age of forty or fifty, come to a standstill in their mental reaching out. Don't think that you must "begin to take in sail," to stop growing, stop progressing, just because you have gotten along in years. By this method of reasoning you will decline rapidly. Never allow yourself to get out of the habit of being young. Do not say that you cannot do this or that as you once did. Live the life that belongs to youth. Do not be afraid of being a boy or girl again in spirit, no matter how many years you have lived. Carry yourself so that you will not suggest old age in any of its phases. Remember it is the stale mind, the stale mentality, that ages the body. Keep growing, keep interested in everything about you.

It has been shown that the conviction that one is going to die at about a certain time, a certain age, tends to bring about the expected dissolution by strangling the life processes.

If you wish to retain your youth, forget unpleasant experiences, disagreeable incidents. A lady eighty years old was recently asked how she managed to keep herself so youthful. She replied: "I know how to forget disagreeable things."

No one can remain youthful who does not continue to grow, and no one can keep growing who does not keep alive his interest in the great world about him. We are so constituted that we draw a large part of our nourishment from others. No man can isolate himself, can cut himself off from his fellows, without shrinking in his mental stature. The mind that is not constantly reaching out for the new, as well as keeping in touch with the old, soon reaches its limit of growth.

Nothing else is easier than for a man to age. All he has to do is to think he is growing old; to expect it, to fear it, and prepare for it; to compare himself with others of the same age who are prematurely old and to assume that he is like them.

To think constantly of the "end," to plan for death, to prepare and provide for declining years, is simply to acknowledge that your powers are waning, that you are losing your grip upon life. Such thinking tends to weaken your hold upon the life principle, and your body gradually corresponds with your conviction.

The very belief that our powers are waning; the consciousness that we are losing strength, that our vitality is lessening; the conviction that old age is settling upon us and that our life forces are gradually ebbing away, has a blighting, shrivelling influence upon the mental faculties and functions; the whole character deteriorates under this old-age belief.

The result is that we do not use or develop the age-resisting forces within us. The refreshening, renewing, resisting powers of the body are so reduced and impaired by the conviction that we are getting on in years and cannot stand what we once could, that we become an easy prey to disease and all sorts of physical infirmities.

The mental attitude has everything to do with the hastening or the retarding of the old-age condition.

Dr. MetchnikorT, of the Pasteur Institute in Paris, says that men should live at least one hundred and twenty years. There is no doubt that, as a race, we shorten our lives very materially through our false thinking, our bad living, and our old-age convictions.

A few years ago the London Lancet, the highest medical authority in the world, gave a splendid illustration of the power of the mind to keep the body young. A young woman, deserted by her lover, became insane. She lost all consciousness of the passing of time. She believed her lover would return, and for years she stood daily before her window watching for him. When over seventy years of age, some Americans, including physicians, who saw her, thought she was not over twenty. She did not have a single gray hair, and no wrinkles or other signs of age were visible. Her skin was as fair and smooth as a young girl's. She did not age because she believed she was still a girl. She did not count her birthdays or worry because she was getting along in years. She was thoroughly convinced that she was still living in the very time that her lover left her. This mental belief controlled her physical condition. *She was just as old as she thought she was.* Her conviction outpictured itself in her body and kept it youthful. It is an insult to your Creator that your brain should begin to ossify, that your mental powers should begin to decline when you have only reached the half-century milestone. You ought then to be in your youth. What has the appearance of old age to do with youth? What have gray hair, wrinkles, and other evidences of age to do with youth? Mental power should constantly increase. There should be no decline in years. Increasing wisdom and power should be the only signs that you have lived long, that you have been many years on this planet. Strength, beauty, magnificence, superiority, not weakness, uselessness, decrepitude, should characterize a man who has lived long.

As long as you hold the conviction that you are sixty, you will look it. Your thought will outpicture itself in your face, in your whole appearance. If you hold the old-age ideal, the old-age conviction, your expression must correspond. The body is the bulletin board of the mind.

On the other hand, if you think of yourself as perpetually young, vigorous, robust, and buoyant, because every cell in the body is constantly being renewed, decrepitude will not get hold of you.

If you would retain your youth, you must avoid the enemies of youth, and there are no greater enemies than the convictions of age and the gradual loss of interest in things, especially in youthful amusements and in the young life about you. When you are no longer interested in the hopes and ambitions of young people; when you decline to enter into their sports, to romp and play with children, you confess in effect that you are growing old; that you are beginning to harden; that your youthful spirits are drying up, and that the juices of your younger days are evaporating. Nothing helps more to the perpetuation of youth than much association with the young.

A man quite advanced in years was asked not long ago how he retained such a youthful appearance in spite of his age. He said that he had been the principal of a high school for over thirty years; that he loved to enter into the life and sports of the young people and to be one of them in their ambitions and interests. This, he said, had kept his mind centred on youth, progress, and abounding life, and the old-age thought had had no room for entrance.

There is not even a suggestion of age in this man's conversation or ideas, and there is a life, a buoyancy about him which is wonderfully refreshing.

There must be a constant activity in the mind that would not age. "Keep growing or die" is nature's motto, a motto written all over everything in the universe.

Hold stoutly to the conviction that it is natural and right for you to remain young. Constantly repeat to yourself that it is wrong, wicked for you to grow old in appearance; that weakness and decrepitude could not have been in the Creator's plan for the man made in His image of perfection; that it must have been acquired – the result of wrong race and individual training and thinking.

Constantly affirm: "I am always well, always young, I cannot grow old except by producing the old-age conditions through my thought. The Creator intended me for continual growth, perpetual advancement and betterment, and I am not going to allow myself to be cheated out of my birthright of perennial youth."

No matter if people do say to you: "You are getting along in years," "You are beginning to show signs of age." Just deny these appearances. Say to yourself: "Principle does not age, Truth does not grow old. I am Principle. I am Truth." Never go to sleep with the old-age picture or thought in your mind. It is of the utmost importance to make yourself feel young at night; to erase all signs, convictions, and feelings of age; to throw aside every care and worry that would carve its image on your brain and express itself in your face. The worrying mind actually generates calcareous matter in the brain and hardens the cells.

You should fall asleep holding those desires and ideals uppermost in the mind which are dearest to you; which you are the most anxious to realize. As the mind continues to work during sleep, these desires and ideals are thus intensified and increased. It is well known that impure thoughts and desires work terrible havoc then. Purity of thought, loftiness of purpose, the highest possible aims, should dominate the mind when you fall asleep.

When you first wake in the morning, especially if you have reached middle life or later, picture the youthful qualities as vividly as possible. Say to yourself: "I am young, always young – strong – buoyant. I cannot grow old and decrepit, because in the truth of my being I am divine, and Divine Principle cannot age. It is only the negative in me, the unreality, that can take on the appearance of age."

The great thing is to make the mind create the youth pattern instead of the old-age pattern. As the sculptor follows the model which he holds in the mind, so the life processes reproduce in the body the pattern which is in our thought, our conviction.

We must get rid of the idea embedded in our very nature that the longer we live, the more experiences we have, the more work we do, the more inevitably we wear out and become old, decrepit, and useless. We must learn that living, acting, experiencing, should not exhaust life but create more life. It is a law that action increases force. Where, then, did the idea come from that man should wear out through action?

As a matter of fact, Nature has bestowed upon us perpetual youth, the power of perpetual renewal. There is not a single cell in our bodies that can possibly become old; the body is constantly being made new through cell-renewal; and as the cells of these parts of the body that are most active are renewed oftenest, it must follow that the ageproducing process is largely artificial and unnatural.

Physiologists tell us that the tissue cells of some muscles are renewed every few hours, others every few days or weeks. The cells of the bone tissues are slower of renewal, but some authorities estimate that eighty or ninety per cent of all the cells in the body of a person of ordinary activity are entirely renewed in from six to twelve months.

Scientists have proved beyond question that the chemistry of the body has everything to do with the perpetuation of youthful conditions. Every discordant thought produces a chemical change in the cells, introducing foreign substances and causing reaction which is injurious to the integrity of the cells.

The impression of age is thus made upon new cells. This impression is the thought. If the thought is old, the age impress appears upon the cells. If the spirit of youth dominates the thought, the impression upon the cells is youthful. In other words, the processes which result in age cannot possibly operate except through the mind, and the billions of cells composing the body are instantly affected by every thought that passes through the brain.

Putting old thoughts into a new set of cells is like putting new wine into old bottles. They don't agree; they are natural enemies. The result is that two-year-old cells are made to look fifty, sixty, or more years old, according to the thought.

It is marvellous how quickly old thoughts can make new cells appear old.

All discordant and antagonistic thought materially interferes with the laws of reconstruction and self-renewal going on in the body, and the great thing is, therefore, to form thought habits which will harmonize with this law of rejuvenation – perpetual renewal.

Hard, selfish, worry, and fear thoughts, and vicious habits of all kinds, produce the appearance of age and hasten its coming.

Pessimism is one of the worst enemies of youth. The pessimist ages prematurely because his mind dwells upon the black, discordant, and diseased side of things. The pessimist does not progress, does not face toward youth; he goes backward, and this retrogression is fatal to youthful conditions. Brightness, cheerfulness, hopefulness characterize youth.

Everything that is abnormal tends to produce old-age conditions. No one can remain young, no matter to what expedients he may resort to enable him to erase the marks of age, who worries and indulges in excessive passion. The mental processes produce all sorts of things, good or bad, according to the pattern in the mind.

Selfishness is abnormal and tends to harden and dry up the brain and nerve cells. We are so constituted that we must be good to be happy, and happiness spells youthfulness. Selfishness is an enemy of happiness because it violates the veryfundamental principle of our being – justice, fairness. We protest against it, we instinctively despise and think less of ourselves for practicing it. It does not tend to produce health, harmony, or a sense of well-being, because it does not harmonize with the fundamental principle of our being.

With many people, old age is a perpetual horror, which destroys comfort and happiness and makes life a tragedy, which, but for it, might have been a perpetual joy.

Many wealthy people do not really enjoy their possessions because of that awful consciousness that they may at any moment be forced to leave everything.

Discordant thought of every kind tends to shorten life.

As long as you think old, hard, grasping, envious thoughts, nothing in the world can keep you from growing old. As long as you harbor these enemies of youth, you cannot remain in a youthful condition. New thoughts create new life; old thoughts – canned, stereotyped thoughts – are injurious to growth, and anything which stops growth helps the aging processes.

Whatever thought dominates the mind at any-time is constantly modifying, changing the life ideal, so that every suggestion that comes into the mind from any source is registered in the cell life, etched in the character, and outpictured in the expression and appearance. If the ideal of continual youth, of a body in a state of perpetual rejuvenation, dominates the mind, it neutralizes the aging processes. All of the body follows the dominating thought, motive and feeling, and takes on its expression. For example, a man who is constantly worrying, fretting, a victim of fear, cannot possibly help outpicturing this condition in his body. Nothing in the world can counteract this hardening, aging, ossifying process but a complete reversal of the thought, so that the opposite ideas dominate. The effect of the mind on the body is always absolutely scientific. It follows an inexorable law.

There is a power of health latent in every cell of the body which would always keep the cell in harmony and preserve its integrity if the thought were right. This latent power of health in the cell can be so developed by right thinking and living as to retard very materially the aging processes.

One of the most effective means of developing it is to keep cheerful and optimistic. As long as the mind faces the sun of life it will cast no shadow before it.

Hold ever before you, like a beacon light, the youth ideal – strength, buoyancy, hopefulness, expectancy. Hold persistently to the thought that your body is the last two years' product; that there may not be in it a single cell more than a year and a half old ; that it is constantly young because it is perpetually being renewed and that, therefore, it ought to look fresh and youthful.

Constantly say to yourself: "If Nature makes me a new body every few months, comparatively, if the billions of tissue cells are being perpetually renewed, if the oldest of these cells are, perhaps, rarely, if ever, more than two years old, why should they appear to be sixty or seventy-five?" A two-year-old cell could not look like a seventyyear-old cell of its own accord, but we know from experience that the old-age conviction can make these youthful cells look very old. If the body is always young, it should always look young; and it would if we did not make it look old by stamping old age upon it. We Americans seem very adept in putting the old-age stamp upon new tissue cells. Yet it is just as easy to form the youthful-thought habit as the old-age-thought habit. If you would keep young, you must learn the secret of self -rejuvenation, self-refreshment, selfrenewal, in your thought, in your work. Hard thoughts, too serious thoughts, mental confusion, excitement, worry, anxiety, jealousy, the indulgence of explosive passions, all tend to shorten life.

You will find a wonderful rejuvenating power in the cultivation of faith in the *immortal Principle of health in every atom of your being.*

We are all conscious that there is something in us which is never sick and which never dies, *something which* connects us with the Divine. There is a wonderful healing influence in holding the consciousness of this great truth.

Some people are so constituted that they perpetually renew themselves. They do not seem to get tired or weary of their tasks, because their minds are constantly refreshing themselves. They are self-lubricators, self-renewers. To keep from aging, we must keep the picture of youth in all its beauty and glory impressed upon the mind. It is impossible to appear youthful, to be young, unless we feel young.

Without realizing it, most people are using the old-age thought as a chisel to cut a little deeper the wrinkles. Their old-age thought is stamping itself upon the new cells only a few months old, so that they very soon look to be forty, fifty, sixty, or seventy years old.

Never allow yourself to think of yourself as growing old. Constantly affirm, if you feel yourself aging, "I am young because I am perpetually being renewed ; my life comes new every moment from the Infinite Source of life. I am new every morning and fresh every evening because I live, move, and have my being in Him who is the Source of all life." Not only affirm this mentally, but verbally when you can. Make this picture of perpetual renewal, constant refreshment, re-creation, so vivid, that you will feel the thrill of youthful renewal through your entire system. Under no circumstances allow the old-age thought and suggestion to remain in the mind. Remember that it is what you feel, what you are convinced of, that will be outpictured in your body. If you think you are aging, if you walk, talk, dress, and act like an old person, these conditions will be outpictured in your expression, face, manner, and body generally.

Youthful thought should be a life habit. Cling to the thought that the truth of your being can never age, because it is Divine Principle. Picture the cells of the body being constantly made over. Hold this perpetual-renewal picture in your mind, and the old-age thought, the old-age conviction will become inoperative.

The new youth-thought habit will drive out the old-age-thought habit. If you can only feel your whole body being perpetually made over, constantly renewed, you will keep the body young, fresh.

There is a tremendous youth-retaining power in holding high ideals and lofty sentiments. The spirit cannot grow old while one is constantly aspiring to something better, higher, nobler. Employment which develops the higher self; the frequent dwelling upon lofty themes and high purposes – all are powerful preservatives of youth. It is senility of the soul that makes people old.

The living of life should be a perpetual joy. Youth and joy are synonymous. If we do not enjoy life, if we do not feel that it is a delight to be alive, if we do not look upon our work as a grand privilege, we shall age prematurely.

Live always in a happy mental-attitude. Live in the ideal, and the aging-processes cannot get hold of you. It is the ideal that keeps one young. When we think of age, we think of weakness, decrepitude, imperfection; we do not think of wholeness, vigor. Every time you think of yourself make a vivid mental picture of your ideal self as the very picture of youth, of health and vigor. Think health. Feel the spirit of youth and hope surging through your body. Form the most perfect picture of physical manhood or womanhood that is possible to the human mind.

The elixir of youth which alchemists sought so long in chemicals, we find lies in ourselves. The secret is in our own mentality. Perpetual rejuvenation is possible only by right thinking. We look as old as we think and feel because it is thought and feeling that change our appearance.

Let us put beauty into our lives by thinking beautiful thoughts, building beautiful ideals, and picturing beautiful things in our imagination.

I know of no remedy for old-age conditions so powerful as love – love for our work, love for our fellow-men, love for everything.

It is the most powerful life-renewer, refreshener, re-creator, known. Love awakens the noblest sentiments, the finest sensibilities, the most exquisite qualities in man.

Try to find and live in the soul of things, to see the best in everybody. When you think of a person, hold in your mind the ideal of that person – that which God meant him to be – not the deformed, weak, ignorant creature which vice and wrong living may have made. This habit of refusing to see anything but the ideal will not only be a wonderful help to others, but also to yourself. Refuse to see deformity or weakness anywhere, but hold persistently your highest ideals. Other things being equal, it is the cleanest, purest mind that lives longest.

Harmony, peace, and serenity are absolutely necessary to perpetuate youthful conditions. All discord, all unbalanced mental operations, tend to produce aging conditions. The contemplation of the eternal verities enriches the ideals and freshens life because it destroys fear, uncertainty, and worry by adding assurance and certainty to life.

Old-age conditions can only exist in cells which have become deteriorated and hardened by wrong thinking and vicious living. Unrestrained passion or fits of temper burn out the cells very rapidly.

People who are very useful, who are doing their work grandly, growing vigorously, retain their youthful appearance. We can form the habit of staying young just as well as the habit of growing old.

Increasing power and wisdom ought to be the only sign of our long continuance on this earth. We ought to do our best work after fifty, or even after sixty or seventy; and if the brain is kept active, fresh, and young, and the brain cells are not ruined by too serious a life, by worry, fear, selfishness, or disease, the mind will constantly increase in vigor and power.

If we are convinced that the life processes can perpetuate youth instead of age, they will obey the command. The fact that man's sin, his ignorance of true living, made the threescore years, with the possible addition of ten more, the average limit of life centuries ago, is no reason why any one in this man-emancipating age should narrow himself to this limit.

An all-wise and benevolent Creator could not make us with such a great yearning for long life, a longing to remain young, without any possibility of realizing it. The very fact of this universal protest in all human beings against the enormous dispropor-tion between the magnitude of our mission upon earth and the shortness of the time and the meagreness of the opportunities for carrying it out; the universal yearning for longevity; and all analogy in the animal kingdom, all point to the fact that man was not only intended for a much longer life, but also for a much greater freedom from the present old-age weaknesses and handicaps.

There is not the slightest indication in the marvellous mechanism of man that he was intended to become weak, crippled, and useless after a comparatively few years. Instead, all the indications are toward progress into a larger, completer, fuller manhood, greater power. A dwarfed, weak, useless man was never in the Creator's plan. Retrogression is contrary to all principle and law. Progress, perpetual enlargement, growth, are the truth of man. The Creator never made anything for retrogression; it is contrary to the very nature of Deity. "Onward and upward" is written upon every atom in the universe. Imagine the Creator fashioning a man in his own likeness for only a few years of activity and growth, and then – retrogression, crippled helplessness! There is nothing of God in this picture. Whatever the Deity makes bears the stamp of perpetual progress, everlasting growth. There is no going backward in His plans, everything moves forward to one eternal divine purpose. A decrepit, helpless old man or woman is a burlesque of the human being God made. His image does not deteriorate or go backward, but moves forever onward, eternally upward. If human beings could only once grasp this idea, that the reality of them is divine, and that divinity does not go backward or grow old, they would lose all sense of fear and worry, all enemies of their progress and happiness would slink away, and the aging processes would cease.

The coming man will not grow old. Perpetual youth is his destiny.

The time will come when people will look upon old age as an unreality, a negative, a mere phantom of the real man. The rose that fades is not the real rose. The real rose is the ideal – the idea which pushes out a new one every time we pluck the one that fades.

The real man is God's ideal, and in the light of the new day that is dawning man will glimpse that perfect ideal. He will know the truth, and the truth will make him free. In that new day he will cast from him the hampering, age-worn vestures woven in the thought-loom of mankind through the centuries, and stand erect – the perfect being, the ideal man.

www.ingramcontent.com/pod-product-compliance
Lightning Source LLC
Chambersburg PA
CBHW071752020426
42331CB00008B/2285